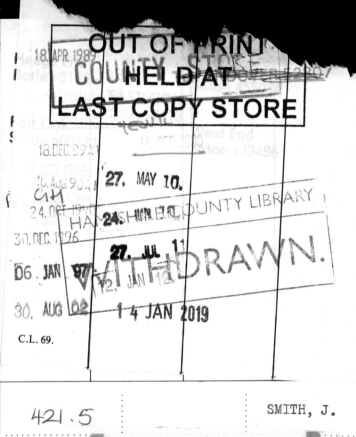

C.7.68.

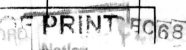

Simple
Phonetics
for Teachers

Jean Smith and Margaret Bloor

Simple Phonetics for Teachers

METHUEN · LONDON

First published in 1985 by
Methuen & Co. Ltd
11 New Fetter Lane,
London EC4P 4EE

© 1985 Jean Smith
and Margaret Bloor

British Library
Cataloguing in
Publication Data

Smith, Jean
Simple phonetics for teachers.
1. English language – Phonetics
I. Title
II. Bloor, Margaret
421'.5   PE1135

ISBN 0-416-39810-3

Typeset in Great Britain by
Rowland Phototypesetting Ltd,
Bury St Edmunds, Suffolk
and printed by
Richard Clay (The Chaucer Press) Ltd,
Bungay, Suffolk

Contents

Foreword:
Why phonetics?

We feel the following story is a good example of the value of phonetics in the teaching of children with specific learning difficulties.

John came for therapy with a reading age of about 6 years and no spelling age at all. His chronological age at the time was 10.6 and the School Child Psychologist had given him an IQ of well over 130.

After nine months of weekly sessions of basic phonic work presented in a multisensory way, John had improved to a reading and spelling age of just over 8 years. John's father was a night worker and so was able to sit in on his lessons and he worked daily with John for a short time, reinforcing the week's lesson and revising past work. Initially John had a lot of difficulty with p/b reversals, but over the months this had disappeared.

The words being studied in one particular lesson were those ending in 'ssion', for example 'mission' and 'transmission' (he was interested in cars). The word 'admission' was dictated and John wrote 'abmission'. His father and the therapist exchanged despairing looks over his head. 'Oh dear – he's reversing again and I did think we'd sorted that one out!' they both thought. Then the therapist had an idea and she asked John to say the word. 'Abmission', he said. 'I thought it came from abmit – you know, abmit one to the football match.'

Much time could have been wasted chasing the reversal red herring. Work could have gone on with directional confusions, talking about the sound /b/ and its symbol, talking about beds, or small 'b' being half of a capital 'B', etc. As it happened, John was assimilating the /d/ forward to a /b/ because of the bilabial that followed it. He had no visual memory of the word (that was his problem) and had always understood those around him to say 'abmit', as indeed they probably did! On investigation it turned out that he also thought he abmired people, and that the man who held high office in the Navy was an Abmiral!

The therapist made a mental note to do some work on 'ad' as a prefix and to look at words where /t/ and /d/ were followed by both bilabials and velars. Did he say 'upmost' or 'oupboard motor'? This was, after all, the same chap who thought there was a metal called 'tim' because the biscuits were kept in a 'tim box'.

Phonetic symbols for English transcription

Voiced

i:	feet	/fi:t/
ɪ	pit	/pɪt/
e	red	/red/
æ	bat	/bæt/
ɑː	hard	/hɑːd/
ɒ	hot	/hɒt/
ɔː	lord	/lɔːd/
ʊ	good	/gʊd/
u:	food	/fu:d/
ʌ	bun	/bʌn/
ɜː	bird	/bɜːd/
ə	paper	/peɪpə/
	(the 'schwa' sound)	
eɪ	date	/deɪt/
əʊ	boat	/bəʊt/
aɪ	time	/taɪm/
aʊ	cow	/kaʊ/
ɔɪ	coin	/kɔɪn/
ɪə	dear	/dɪə/
ɛə	care	/kɛə/
ʊə	pure	/pjʊə/
ḷ	battle	/bætḷ/
ṇ	flatten	flætṇ/
b	bark	/bɑːk/
d	date	/deɪt/
g	gun	/gʌn/

dʒ	jug	/dʒʌg/
v	vote	/vəʊt/
ð	this	/ðɪs/
z	nose	/nəʊz/
ʒ	measure	/meʒə/
m	mother	/mʌðə/
n	nine	/naɪn/
ŋ	singing	/sɪŋɪŋ/
l	late	/leɪt/
r	rat	/ræt/
j	you	/ju:/
w	wind	/wɪnd/

Voiceless

p	pet	/pet/
t	top	/tɒp/
k	cake	/keɪk/
tʃ	church	/tʃɜːtʃ/
f	face	/feɪs/
θ	thin	/θɪn/
s	sit	/sɪt/
ʃ	ship	/ʃɪp/
h	hat	/hæt/

You will notice there is no x as this sound is /ks/. Similarly, q is /kw/ and c is either /k/ or /s/.

Acknowledgements

The authors would like to thank J. D. O'Connor, Emeritus Professor of Phonetics, University College London, for fostering Jean Smith's initial interest in this subject and for the generous help he has given since.

They would also like to acknowledge the free exchange of ideas and information which took place during their time at the Dyslexia Clinic in St Bartholomew's Hospital, London.

1 Introduction

We recognize that a visual approach to learning to read and spell is far more exciting and less complicated than a phonic approach. However, in spite of all its difficulties, it remains a fact that there are some children who will learn to read and spell only if they are taught using a structured phonic programme in a multisensory way. These children seem to need the support of this approach to get them started, although they often develop more visual skills at a later stage.

Many children with specific learning difficulties endeavour to help themselves with a 'do-it-yourself' phonic method. The pitfalls that await them are many, and this book attempts to draw the attention of parents and teachers to the sort of difficulties a child will encounter and to explain the more common errors he will make. Spellings which seem careless can, in fact, be well thought out and phonetically observant attempts to reproduce the sounds the child actually hears and not the sounds we think he hears.

Before embarking on any remedial teaching programme, an attempt should be made to understand the reasons for the child's failure to read and spell. It is acknowledged that these reasons can be very complicated and many of them fall outside the scope of this book. However, in our experience there are some children who have great difficulty in the visual sphere, whereas the difficulties of others are of an acoustic nature (some, of course, have difficulties in both areas!). In addition, spatial, motor and sequential difficulties may overlap in different combinations and this can account for the variety of problems presented.

To generalize, the child with problems of an acoustic nature can be defined:

This child has a deep language problem. Even though the child's auditory acuity may be adequate, he may have poor auditory perception and discrimination skills. He may be unable to remember sounds long enough to reproduce them accurately and he will, therefore, mispronounce consonants and polysyllabic words. He may confuse the sounds of the back vowels /ɒ/ and /ɔː/ and the front vowels /ɪ/ and /e/ or /æ/ and /ʌ/. He may not be able to discriminate between voiced and voiceless sounds. He will not hear devoicing, aspiration and vowel shortening clues. He is difficult to teach to read and often learns to read through writing. His inability to read holds him back in subjects at which he might excel – practical subjects, art and design and subjects requiring scientific or mathematical skills.

He may have some visual memory but without the support of the ability to discriminate, remember and reproduce sounds he will quickly get into difficulties. As he either does not hear or cannot reproduce the sounds of a word in an ordered form, his spellings will sometimes be quite bizarre. In addition, his syntax will be poor and he will have difficulty telling a coherent story or writing an essay which will read well.

He may also be hesitant and rather monosyllabic in his speech. When explaining something he may know what he wants to say but find it difficult to choose the right words. He may, therefore, raise his hand in class in response to a question but be unable to produce his answer if called upon.

He may not be able to recite the days of the week; the alphabet and multiplication tables may be almost impossible. Later in his school career he will have great trouble taking notes in class because he will not be able to listen and write at the same time. He may contribute very little orally in class but be interested in the lesson and able to understand it. On the WISC intelligence scale for children he will have a low verbal score.

The child who has difficulties in the visual sphere:

This child can express himself well orally but seems unable to get it down on paper. He is a great talker but lacks visual recall of words.

He may have good visual acuity but poor visual perception and discrimination and also a poor memory for the sequence of letters within the word. He may have difficulty recognizing that 'm' is not 'n'; 'pne' is not 'pen'; 'was' is not 'saw'. He may miss commas and full stops when reading; when writing he will, in addition, miss capital letters and double consonants. He may transpose letters within words, and read and write 'form' for 'from'. He may omit phonemes and graphemes, reading and writing 'sting' for 'string'. Conversely, he may add them. He may omit prepositions and conjunctions, which will make his text very difficult to read. His lack of visual memory will even hamper him when copying from a book or the chalkboard – he will need to refer back constantly and will lose his place.

His imaginative writing skills may be above average but his work will be marred by poor spelling.

When spelling, the child must either remember what the whole word looks like or be able to appreciate the relationship between sound and symbol and build it. If he has a poor visual memory, he will have no means of telling which words are wrongly spelt – especially if they are phonetically acceptable to him. If he is relying on the sound of the word to recall its spelling he must cope with many difficulties. Vowels are distorted in unstressed syllables. In rapid speech some phonemes are affected by their neighbours, others are left out altogether and some are not properly pro-nounced at the end of words. In some words whole syllables are omitted. It can also be difficult for the child to recognize variations of the same phoneme. He will need help to guide him through these difficulties and a phonic approach will be of most help to him.

It seems, then, that a phonic based programme, carefully struc-tured and taught in a multisensory manner is one of the more successful methods of teaching both these types of children as well as those with difficulties in both areas. It can give them the confidence to make a fresh beginning. However, if this approach is to be used, it is important that the teacher understands the sounds she is dealing with. These are her tools and it is important that she has a sure command of them. If the teacher fully understands how we speak and can appreciate the tiny perceptual clues by which we automatically learn to differentiate between similarly articulated sounds, she will be in a much better position to understand the child and sympathize with him when he writes 'bed' instead of 'pet'.

The listening of most literate adults is so closely linked with their knowledge of the written word that they can be totally misled into thinking they are hearing sounds which are not, in fact, being made. Although optical illusions are readily accepted, acoustical illusions are more difficult to accept and most people find it hard to believe that they *hear spelling*.

This book sets out to help teachers and parents to understand the basics of phonetics so that they may listen to speech in a more informed way and so be able to understand more fully the difficulties encountered by the child who has no alternative to the phonic approach to learning to spell. It should be understood, however, that this book is not a complete course in phonetics. The speech described is largely restricted to RP (Received Pronunciation); the whole complex study of intonation patterns has been omitted, together with the phonemes (sounds) of other languages and many other facets of a detailed study of phonetics. We have extracted facts which we find relevant and have tried to present them simply. We apologize to 'real phoneticians' for omissions or generalizations which might offend them. Our intention is to cover only areas that have proved valuable in our own work.

2 Changes in sound

It is presumed that the reader will have some knowledge of the movements of the organs of articulation in the realization of English phonemes and that the terms PLOSIVE, FRICATIVE, NASAL, LATERAL, etc. will convey meaning. However, should the reader require them, diagrams and simple explanations of how individual sounds of speech are made, together with a diagram showing the nasal cavity, the alveolar ridge, velum, etc., can be found in chapter four.

HOW SOUNDS ARE MADE

When air passes from the lungs, through the vocal folds, and emerges from the mouth (or nose) a sound is produced. Its nature is determined by several factors:

1 whether or not the vocal folds vibrate as the air passes through them;
2 the position of the velum (soft palate);
3 the movement of the tongue;
4 the shape of the lips.

The linking of individual phonemes constitutes speech which is a continuous exercise. Each phoneme (sound) can be affected by its neighbour and slight variations will occur.

When the vocal folds do not vibrate as the air passes through them the phoneme produced is VOICELESS. When they do vibrate the phoneme is VOICED. However, this vibration does not begin or end abruptly. VOICING can carry on from one sound to the next, slightly modifying a neighbouring voiceless sound. By the same token, the close proximity of a voiceless phoneme can make a voiced phoneme become slightly devoiced or shorten its duration.

The movements of the velum (soft palate) which control the flow of air through the nose are also made in a fluid way and are not abrupt so the surrounding phonemes can be slightly nasalized.

In the rest of this chapter an attempt will be made to explain some of the more common modifications and their relevance to spelling mistakes.

PLOSIVES

PLOSIVES are made by the air from the lungs building up behind a barrier formed by closed lips or the tongue touching the roof of the mouth. This closure is released suddenly and the air escapes with PLOSION.

Of the six English plosives, three are voiced – the bilabial /b/, the alveolar /d/ and the velar /g/. Each of these has a voiceless partner – the bilabial /p/, the alveolar /t/ and the velar /k/ (spelt c or k).

	Bilabial (lip sounds)	Alveolar (tongue behind front teeth)	Velar (back of tongue raised to soft palate)
Vocal fold vibration	b	d	g
No vibration	p	t	k

/b/ Voiced bilabial plosive

Although the distinction between /b/ and /p/ is generally taken to be one of voice, in fact it is rare for any voiced plosive, i.e. /b/, /d/ or /g/ to be fully voiced at the beginning or end of a word. A child may have great difficulty in relating the devoiced phoneme he hears in a word to the fully voiced sound he has learned in isolation. He may, in fact, write its voiceless equivalent.

The following voicing diagram gives an example of devoicing. The vibrating line represents voicing.

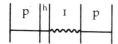

If the /b/ phonemes in this word are almost completely devoiced, how do most of us perceive that the word is 'bib' and not 'pip'? First let us look at the /b/ at the beginning of the word. The difference between the two bilabials /p/ and /b/ in this situation in a word is perceived by the presence or absence of ASPIRATION.

All that has been said of /b/ could equally be said of /d/. The same rules apply.

ASPIRATION

ASPIRATION is a tiny puff of air that accompanies the three voiceless plosives /p/, /t/ and /k/ when they are found at the beginning of an accented syllable and before a vowel. Also, but to a lesser degree, when they are found word finally. This puff of air can be shown on the voicing diagram by a small [^{h}].

The voiceless plosives are made with more force of air and are termed FORTIS. The voiced plosives have less force and are termed LENIS. The presence of a *puff of air*, together with the relative force of the fortis /p/, is the perceptual clue to the difference between /p/ and /b/ at the beginning of the words 'pip' and 'bib' (or any other CVC – consonant vowel consonant – word that starts with a plosive).

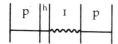 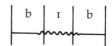

Plosives word finally

Aspiration at the end of a word is not likely to be so strong and may be completely absent, so another perceptual clue is more important here. The three voiceless plosives /p/, /t/ and /k/ tend to shorten the DURATION of the preceding vowel. The voicing diagram could be exaggerated to look like this:

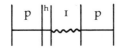   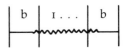

Practise saying words with p/b, t/d and k/g finally and try to perceive the different duration of the vowel. Try saying 'flap' and 'flab' and you will hear that the /æ/ is clipped short by the /p/. Then try 'mat' and 'mad' and 'luck' and 'lug'.

We rely heavily on the duration of the vowel for perception of the final consonant. In fact, so adept are we at the skill of listening for the duration of the vowel and choosing the right final phoneme, that a roomful of adults can have almost 100 per cent success at writing lists of words even if that final phoneme is *not actually* pronounced, providing the length of the vowel is slightly exaggerated when the words end in /b/, /d/ or /g/. At the end of this type of word it is the vowel duration we are listening to and not the voiced/voiceless relationship of the final phoneme at all.

A child with poor perceptual ability may miss these clues and could write the words 'bib' or 'pip' as 'bip' or 'pib'. Many children are intrigued by snippets of this sort of information and enjoy playing games designed to develop their perception. They can be told to listen to words ending in 'p' or 'b'. The final letter is not pronounced – they have to guess that.

    mo . . . (b)
    mo (p)
    ca (p)
    ca . . . (b)
    ri . . . (b)
    ri (p)

The same game can be played with t/d and ck/g.

Other factors that confuse matters when plosives occur at the end of a word are:

1 the English habit of using a glottal stop (closure of the vocal folds) instead of the final voiceless phoneme, or
2 the habit of failing to release the plosion of the final phoneme at all. We make the oral closure either with the lips as in /p/ or /b/, or with the tongue as in /t/, /d/, /k/ or /g/. Then we fail to release the air with plosion and allow the velum (soft palate) to lower and the air to

escape gently through the nose. Given that this inaudible release of the final phoneme takes place – either in the teacher's speech or in the child's sub-vocalizing – the words 'pip', 'pit' and 'pick' might sound very similar. We would see the lip closure for 'pip', of course. Similar auditory confusions could be made between 'rub', 'rud' and 'rug'.

If the child cannot quite hear that final sound he will be at a loss to know how to finish his word even if he does realize that the word is incomplete. In this situation he often falls back on guesswork.

More about aspiration

Aspiration is used preceding a vowel in an unaccented syllable too, although it is perhaps weaker. In /təmɒrəʊ/ – tomorrow – the /t/ would have only weak aspiration because the stress is on the second syllable. Try saying 'tea' and then 'tomorrow' and see if you can hear the difference in the realization of the /t/.

Weak aspiration, or none, is used intervocalically (between vowels) and ending a stressed syllable as in the word /peɪpə/ – 'paper'. Here the first /p/ would be strongly aspirated and the second would have weaker aspiration. In practice this might cause the child to write the second /p/ as a /b/.

At the end of a word aspiration is sometimes used and sometimes not, depending entirely on the speaker, thus adding to the child's difficulties.

The mistakes the child is likely to make, then, are obvious. He is likely to confuse all the voiceless/voiced pairs. There are, in addition, extra problems with p/b and to a lesser degree s/z, in that they have visually similar symbols. As many of our children have both auditory and visual memory problems, coupled with directional confusion, it all becomes a bit hit or miss. Sometimes they get it right and sometimes they don't! It is often this variability of performance that finally makes the teacher lose patience. One tends to think that a child is just not trying if he spells correctly at the top of the page and incorrectly at the bottom. To check back and re-read seems to be too much of a chore for these children. Having laboured to write something, it almost seems as if they wish to be finished with it for ever and never have to look at it again.

FRICATIVES

Having considered the phonemes where the air is actually stopped momentarily in the oral cavity, we should now look at the group where a closure is nearly made but enough of a gap is left for the air to pass through with considerable friction.

This group, the FRICATIVES, also appear in voiceless/voiced pairs and so produce confusions. These pairs are:

	Labio dental	Dental	Alveolar	Palato-alveolar
Voiceless	f	θ	s	ʃ
Voiced	v	ð	z	ʒ

To these can be added /tʃ/ as in 'church' and /dʒ/ as in 'judge', where two sounds are released so quickly that they sound like one phoneme. These are called AFFRICATES. The stop is released as a very short fricative.

The confusions are both obvious and not so obvious. The child may hear the voiceless phoneme for the voiced and again the voiced phonemes can be devoiced in certain circumstances. (See *voicing*, p. 13.)

'Th'

One of the less obvious difficulties is the fact that both dental fricatives /θ/ and /ð/ are spelt 'th'. This worries the child who has learnt to expect such distinctly different sounds to have different spellings. Usually, a voiceless phoneme has a different symbol from a voiced phoneme made in the same place of articulation, e.g. p/b, or s/z. With these two, however, /ðɪs/ – 'this' is written with the same initial digraph as /θɪŋ/ – 'thing'.

Plural s

Some children have difficulties with simple plurals. We usually spell them 's' but if that 's' follows a voiced consonant we hear /z/ because we do not bother to stop voicing.

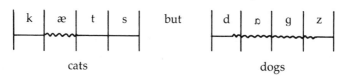

cats   but   dogs

LACK OF ASPIRATION OF VOICELESS PLOSIVES AFTER AN /s/

When we teach the sounds of the voiceless plosives in isolation, /p/, /t/ and /k/, we add aspiration. Indeed it would be difficult not to do so. The child associates the written symbols with their aspirated sounds. However, when the voiceless plosives follow an /s/ they lose this aspiration. In practice this means that:

sp, st, and sk* *or* sc

will all have unaspirated second phonemes and the /p/, /t/ or /k/ immediately begin to sound like their voiced pairs /b/, /d/ and /g/.

sp → sb
st → sd
sc *or* sk → sg

In fact, the /b/, /d/ and /g/ in this situation would be devoiced by the /s/ so the difference between the voiced/voiceless pairs would be neutralized and lost. The opposition between the pairs has gone, and in phonemic transcription (writing in phonemic symbols) it would be perfectly valid to assign the sound to either phoneme. We use 'sp', 'st', 'sc' or 'sk' because *we know how the word is spelt.*

If you say the word 'spin' the /p/ sounds just like a /b/ would sound in the same position and the child who has a poor visual memory of the word and writes 'sbin' is not so very wrong after all – that is what he hears! In fact his writing 'sb' may indicate how acute his auditory perception is. Ours is fogged by our knowledge of spelling and we think we hear 'sp'. He needs to be taught that, whatever he hears, 'sb' is not an acceptable English blend and that the same applies to 'sd' and 'sg'. A voicing diagram for 'pin' and 'spin' would be:

---

*'Sk', of course, will usually be used before 'e', 'i' or 'y' as in 'sketch', 'skill' and 'sky' where a 'c' would sound like /s/. There are a few exceptions to this generalization but not many – 'skull', 'skate' and 'skunk' come to mind.

and it is the loss of that puff of air, or aspiration, that makes the second word sound like 'sbin'. A voicing diagram for 'sbin' would be very similar to that for 'spin'. The visual clues that might help the child, i.e. the closure of the lips, would be the same for /p/ and /b/ too.

A favourite example of how we use our intuitive knowledge of aspiration is in the way we tell the difference between 'that stuff' and 'that's tough'.

In 'stuff' the /t/ is unaspirated and the /s/ is strong.
In 'tough' the /t/ is aspirated and the preceding /s/ is weaker.

The presence or absence of a puff of air, then, is the key factor.

Minor things like puffs of air do not come into the reckoning of the child with perceptual or language problems.

FRICTIONLESS CONTINUANTS

Nasals

The nasals used in English are:

	Bilabial	Alveolar	Velar
	m	n	ŋ

These nasals resemble the voiced plosives /b/, /d/ and /g/ in that a stop is made in the mouth, but they differ in that the velum (soft palate) is LOWERED and the air escapes through the nose, giving the sound nasal resonance. The air escapes freely, so they are classed as CONTINUANTS, and are usually voiced, although voiceless allophones can occur.

Laterals

The lateral /l/ is frictionless too, and so comes into the same category of continuant as the nasals. It is made by the air passing freely over the rim, or rims, of the tongue either on one side or both.

Post alveolar frictionless continuant /r/

Here again the air passes freely over the tongue. In many ways the sound is vowel-like in its realization.

Semi-vowels /j/ and /w/

These two phonemes are also vowel-like in their realization, but are treated as consonants because that is their FUNCTION in the language.

All these phonemes – /l/, /r/, /j/ and /w/ – are usually voiced, although voiceless allophones of them do occur. (See below.)

(The term APPROXIMANT is sometimes used as an alternative to FRICTIONLESS CONTINUANT.)

VOICING

Although we think of certain consonants as VOICED, in some positions in a word, as we have seen, they are only partially voiced or completely devoiced. When we teach these sounds in isolation, of course, we voice them.

When sounds are devoiced within words the perceptual clues we can use to identify them are the presence or absence of ASPIRATION, the FORTIS/LENIS element or the vowel shortening clues. However, our visual memory of how a word is spelt is so strong that these perceptual skills go unnoticed. We do not even realize that we use them.

Some children have very poor visual memories. They cannot see the word in their 'mind's eye', so their teachers must analyse their own perceptual skills in order to understand and help the child develop his. A thorough understanding of the voiced and voiceless elements of the sounds we make will enable the teacher to anticipate and understand a child's mis-spellings and develop a more sympathetic approach to his difficulties.

14   Simple Phonetics for Teachers

We generalize about the English phonemes as follows:

A Voiceless

p   t   k   f   θ (th)   s   ʃ (sh)   tʃ (ch)   h

Some accents show intervocalic voicing (between two vowels). Americans and West Country speakers, for instance, voice the /t/ in 'butter' /bʌdər/. Other people will voice the /h/ in words like 'behave'.

B Voiced in isolation

b   d   g   v   ð (th)   z   ʒ   dʒ

These phonemes are always voiced between vowels or voiced sounds but, as already explained, they can be devoiced at the beginning and end of words and a child may hear the voiceless partner instead. Even more confusion arises in rapid speech. In the word:

d	ɒ	g

dog

the voicing starts late and begins to fade early. In rapid speech if the following word starts with a voiceless sound then the final consonant would be fully devoiced:

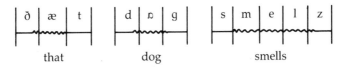

that   dog   smells

However, the /g/ would be fully voiced if a voiced sound follows quickly:

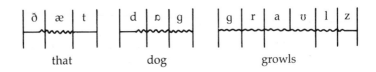

that   dog   growls

In the first instance the child may hear 'that dock smells'. If he is concentrating on simply translating sounds into symbols while writing under pressure, it is possible that he could produce two different spellings for 'dog' in one essay, giving the impression of carelessness.

Consider the sentence 'I have to have another appointment.' The voiceless /t/ may devoice the /v/ of the first 'have' and the child might write 'I haf to have'. There is a difference in meaning of the two words – one implying 'I need' and the other implying possession – so he might not even tie them up. It takes a very understanding teacher to tolerate two different spellings of the same word in the same sentence.

Remember that one factor which helps us to distinguish between a devoiced or partially devoiced phoneme and its voiceless pair is the relative force that accompanies the articulation of the voiceless phoneme. It has more 'puff', but some children simply do not have the ability to make this distinction.

To complicate things still further, when the voiced sounds from this group come together at the end of a word they act as one and the voicing will begin to fade unless the next word begins with a voiced sound. For instance the final consonants /gd/ in the word 'nagged' will be partly devoiced before a pause or a voiceless sound:

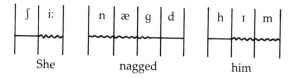

but they are fully voiced if a voiced sound follows:

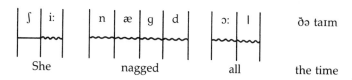

So we see that the same word 'nagged' can sound slightly different when used in varied contexts. In the first example the child might write 'She nat him', hearing the /d/ as a /t/ and possibly not hearing the /g/ at all, as its release would be cut off by the tip of the tongue rising to the alveolar ridge for the /d/. Alternatively, the child could hear the /g/

but be confused by the fact that the voiceless /h/ makes the /d/ sound more like its voiceless partner /t/. He might, therefore, write 'She nag tim'.

C Usually voiced

The phonemes in this group are:

m n ŋ w j r l (/j/ as in /jɪə/ – 'year')

These sounds are usually voiced. Unlike those in group B they are fully voiced word initially and word finally as well as intervocalically. They do appear, however, in clusters or blends and if they follow a voiceless phoneme in that cluster then the whole cluster is rendered voiceless.

In practice this means that the following initial consonant blends all have a devoiced second or third element:

pl, pr, tr, cr, sw, sl, sn, sm, fr, fl, spr, shr, spl, thr, squ, str, scr and tw.

Children are often taught these blends in isolation with the second or third element stressed and voiced (and even with a schwa /ə/ added*). Confusion arises when they do not link the devoiced sounds they hear within a word with the stressed, voiced blend they have been taught. We find examples of such voiceless phonemes (or devoiced phonemes) in the following words.

track [tɹ̥æk]	pray [pɹ̥eɪ]	please [pl̥iːz]
clean [kl̥iːn	twice [tw̥aɪs]	quick [kw̥ɪk]
pew [pj̥uː]	tune [tj̥uːn]	queue [kj̥uː]
splash [spl̥æʃ]	flag [fl̥æg]	squirrel [skw̥ɪrəl]
sly [sl̥aɪ]	swing [sw̥ɪŋ]	smell [sm̥el]
snail [sn̥eɪl]	three [θɹ̥iː]	cry [kɹ̥aɪ]
shrink [ʃɹ̥ɪŋk]	frog [fɹ̥ɒg]	string [stɹ̥ɪŋ]
screw [skɹ̥uː]	spring [spɹ̥ɪŋ]	(The small circle denotes devoicing)

Try saying these words. Then say them again, but this time stop before making the vowel sound. Repeat each blend on its own and

---

*The schwa is a vowel sound used in unstressed syllables, e.g. the initial sound in 'away' /əweɪ/ and the final sound in 'letter' /letə/.

really listen to how it actually sounds and not how you imagine it sounds. It is amazing how it differs from our preconceived notion. /tr/, for example, has two components which differ quite dramatically from their sounds when made separately. Say the word 'track' and then say it again, stopping before the /æ/ sound.

1 The /t/ is not aspirated and is made with the tongue tip touching the alveolar ridge in a post alveolar (towards the back of the ridge) position.
2 The /r/ is usually voiced, but in this blend the /t/ will have rendered it voiceless. It also has a more breathy sound than usual as it is made so quickly after the /t/ that the tongue has not had time to get far away from the ridge and it is realized as a fricative.

The effect is rather like the sound /tʃ/. Certainly small children often use 'ch' instead of 'tr' both in speech and in writing.

When confronted by one of these devoiced consonants the child uses various gambits. He may substitute a similar sounding letter, if there is one, or he may ignore it altogether in the hope that it will go away! Sometimes it lingers around in his mind and he hopefully puts in the odd letter later on in the word just to add to the confusion. If all else fails he may have a long think and then add Magic e* rather hopefully to the end of the word, as he has found that this produces the congratulatory smile of approval in other circumstances.

The nasal phonemes in this group and the lateral /l/ are partially devoiced after a voiceless consonant when they are pronounced syllabically. Small children (and some adults) often insert a schwa /ə/, in which case the voicing will be retained.

Pronunciation 1	Pronunciation 2
[bætn̥] batten	/bætən/
[beɪkn̥] bacon	/beɪkən/
[æpl̥] apple	/æpəl/

The word 'bacon' can even be pronounced [beɪkŋ̊] as the /n/ can assimilate back to /ŋ/. (See *assimilation*, p. 19.)

Devoicing can occur over word boundaries in rapid speech. For instance the final /t/ in the word 'that' might devoice the /w/ in 'that

*Magic e refers to the spelling pattern vowel–consonant–e, as in 'ate', sometimes known as Lengthening e or Silent e but called Magic e throughout this book.

way', [ðæt w̥eɪ] or the /l/ in 'that lot' [ðæt l̥ɒt]. The final /s/ might have the same effect in 'this way' [ðɪs w̥eɪ].

D Always voiced

Vowels and diphthongs are voiced except, very occasionally, in an unstressed syllable between two voiceless phonemes, e.g. the /ə/ in 'success' /səkses/ and 'support' /səpɔːt/.

APPROACH, HOLD AND RELEASE

A sound is identified during a brief holding of the position of the organs of articulation but it can be influenced by the way in which those organs approach that position and by the way in which the flow of air is released afterwards. Each sound has three distinct stages – approach, hold and release.

Lateral approach and release

In the word 'badly' the /d/ is not released by dropping the tongue tip, but the tongue remains touching the ridge until its sides drop to allow the air to escape laterally after the /l/. In 'alter' the tongue tip remains in position but the sides rise and form a stop against the upper molars for the /t/.

Even if the child manages to isolate that /l/ as a separate sound, it can be difficult to relate it to the /l/ he has learnt.

Nasal release

In such words as 'submit' /sʌbmɪt/ the velum (soft palate) rises to shut off the nasal resonators and the lips close for the /b/. The lips remain closed for the /m/ although the velum lowers and allows the air to escape nasally. The /b/, therefore, has a nasal rather than oral release.

In the word 'under' /ʌndə/ the /n/ is made through the nose but the tongue does not leave the alveolar ridge until after the /d/. A child, relying on sub-vocalizing the word to discover its spelling, may not hear the /m/ in the first example nor the /n/ in the second. These nasals may have been reduced to just 'a feeling in his nose' rather than a distinguishable sound.

Vowels

Vowels, too, can sound quite different if they are nasalized. An adjacent /m/, /n/ or /ŋ/ will have this effect. The whole utterance has a fluid continuity and is not executed jerkily. Therefore during the last segment of a vowel the soft palate will start to descend if the oncoming phoneme is a nasal. The /æ/ in 'cat', therefore, will have a different sound from the /æ/ in 'can'. In 'man' both the onset and the end of the vowel would have this influence and the whole vowel will be nasalized. In a detailed phonetic description of the word the vowel would be marked [æ̃].

The nearness of the place of articulation of vowels can also confuse the child. The vowels /ɪ/ and /e/ are close to each other, as are /æ/ and /ʌ/ and these are the most common ones in which mistakes occur. This very slight difference in sound is hard for the child to appreciate.

ASSIMILATION AND ELISION

We now come to the vexed subject of ASSIMILATION. For social reasons many students have a mental barrier to overcome about this. People seem to think that to admit that they assimilate implies 'sloppy speech'. Others delight in recognizing it and enjoy looking for new examples. Assimilation is a simplification of articulation and part of the normal flow of sound that pours forth from humans. We all do it to a greater or lesser degree.

The alveolar phonemes (/t/, /d/, and /n/) are the most likely to assimilate as they are the most unstable.

1 When followed by *any* bilabial /p/, /b/ and /m/, the alveolar phoneme can change to a bilabial and often does. It will, however, retain its voiceless/voiced/nasal pattern. This bilabial is held and not released until the release of the following bilabial.

Alveolar		Bilabial
t	→	p
d	→	b
n	→	m

The following changes are likely to occur in rapid speech.

that pen	/ðæp pen/
that box	/ðæp bɒks/
that man	/ðæp mæn/
bad pain	/bæb peɪn/
bad boy	/bæb bɔɪ/
bad man	/bæb mæn/
thin person	/θɪm pɜːsən/
thin boy	/θɪm bɔɪ/
thin man	/θɪm mæn/

Assimilation also happens within words.

utmost	/ʌpməʊst/
admit	/əbmɪt/
unpick	/ʌmpɪk/

2 When the alveolar is followed by a velar phoneme it also assimilates as follows:

Alveolar		Velar
t	→	k
d	→	g
n	→	ŋ

In rapid speech, the following changes are likely to occur.

white coat	/waɪk kəʊt/
white gloves	/waɪk glʌvz/
good cat	/gʊg kæt/
good girl	/gʊg gɜːl/
tin can	/tɪŋ kæn/
tin god	/tɪŋ gɒd/

Again, this happens frequently within the word. In fact in the word 'thank' /θæŋk/ or 'tingle' /tɪŋgl̩/ one would be unlikely to hear the unassimilated form. No one says /θænk/.

Velar plosives can assimilate right forward to a bilabial position:

| black pen | /blæp pen/ |
| Blackpool | /blæppuːl/ |

and so on.

Assimilated fricatives

The fricatives in the alveolar area are also subject to movement when they are followed by /ʃ/, /ʒ/ or /j/:

| this shoe | /ðɪʃ ʃuː/ |
| these ships | /ðiːʒ ʃɪps/ |

and within a word:

| spaceship | /speɪʃʃɪp/. |

When /j/ follows /s/ and /z/ it may even disappear altogether and we speak of COALESCENT ASSIMILATION. The /s/ and /j/ coalesce into /ʃ/ and the /z/ and /j/ coalesce into /ʒ/:

this year	/ðɪʃ ʃɪə/
last year	/lɑːʃ ʃɪə/
six years	/sɪkʃ ʃɪəz/
was your	/wɒʒɔː/.

Another example of coalescent assimilation would be 'Soviet Union' /səʊvɪətʃuːnɪən/.

Other assimilations

    m plus f or v
    n plus f or v

Here the /n/ or /m/ is made with the top teeth touching the lower lip (a labio-dental allophone for which the phonetic symbol is [ɱ]).

| infant [ɪɱfənt] | involve [ɪɱvɒlv] |
| unfair [ʌɱfɛə] | comfort [kʌɱfət] |

Cockney speech has many examples of assimilation:

what's your name? /wɒtʃə neɪm/	not quite /nɒkwaɪt/
I hate you /aɪ heɪtʃə/	red plum /reb plʌm/
would you /wʊdʒjuː/	in my room /ɪm maɪ rʊm/
not yet /nɒtʃ jet/	thin cotton /θɪŋ kɒtən/.

Assimilation does not have to happen. We tend to change our speech in various situations and some people admit to assimilating all the time, whereas others articulate carefully in public but are more relaxed in their speech at home.

One often finds a child who has an entirely wrong concept of a word because he has never registered its spelling and genuinely believes it to be the assimilated form – the child who thinks that he eats 'hop pot' and that the biscuit tin is made of 'tim' because his mother always refers to it as the 'tim box'.

Elision

Elision is the total omission of a phoneme or a group of phonemes. Some elisions have happened historically and, although we still spell the word with the missing phoneme, we *never* say it. An example of historical elision is the word 'listen'. No one says /lɪsten/ any more and /lɪsən/ is generally heard.

Initial elision	/wr/, /kn/, /gn/ and so on as in 'write', 'know' and 'gnaw'
Medial elision	/t/ is elided in 'fasten', 'listen', 'thistle', 'castle'
	/l/ is elided in 'walk' and 'talk'
Final elision	/mb/ and /mn/ as in 'lamb' and 'hymn'

There are many examples of contextual elision. In this case both elided and unelided forms are heard. Their use will depend on individual speakers and the care with which they are speaking.

last night	/lɑːs naɪt/
Westminster	/wesmɪnstə/
Christmas	/krɪsməs/
last player	/lɑːs pleɪə/
next thing	/neks θɪŋ/
murderer	/mɜːdrə/
literary	/lɪtrɪ/
library	/laɪbrɪ/

half past two   /hɑː pɑːs tuː/
temporary   /temprɪ/

In some cases whole syllables are elided. Small wonder that the child writes 'tempry', etc!

Elision of vowels

Vowels, too, can be elided. The words 'support' and 'sport' can both be articulated similarly but not quite identically, and native English speakers are easily able to sort out which is which by listening to the perceptual clue of the aspiration of the /p/ – [pʰ]. In 'support' – /səpɔːt/ even if the first vowel is elided the /p/ still keeps its aspiration [spʰɔːt]. In 'sport' – [spɔːt] the /s/ has removed that aspiration.

Compound words can be modified by assimilation, elision or both. Take the words 'grandpa' /grændpɑː/ and 'handbag' /hændbæg/. These words are commonly pronounced /græmpɑː/ and /hæmbæg/ with both assimilation and elision.

American visitors to these shores continue to delight us by using unelided forms of English place names:

Worcester   /wɜːsestər/
Gloucester   /glɒsestər/
Salisbury   /sælɪzberiː/
Buckingham   /bʌkɪŋhæm/.

ALLOPHONES

The position in which a sound is made in the word and its situation in relation to the phonemes around it can have quite an effect on the way it is articulated. If you say the word 'eight' /eɪt/ and the word 'eighth' /eɪtθ/, you will feel that the articulation of the /t/ in 'eighth' is made in a more forward position – in fact the tongue tip is against the inside of the upper front teeth. The /θ/ phoneme affects the way in which the /t/ is made and a dental allophone is produced.

Try saying 'key' and 'car'. You will realize that the back of the tongue meets the velum in an advanced position for 'key' and in a retracted position for 'car'.

How is it that these variants are not given the status of separate phonemes?

As English speakers we feel that they are simply variations of the same phoneme. They have a phonetic similarity and their differences occur only because their position in the word has resulted in other close sounds causing changes in the way they are made. If words in which they occur are enunciated slowly and carefully, giving each unit its pure sound, the result would be jerky, difficult to produce and difficult to listen to. Allophones are the result of phonemes' *position* in the word. Each occurs within its given set of circumstances and is not replaced by another variation *in the same position*.

Contrastiveness

The phonemes /t/ and /d/ also have phonetic similarity but we do not feel that they are variations of the same phoneme. They can occur in the same position in a word but their differences do not serve to simplify articulation. They alter the meaning of the word. Pairs of words can be found where one phoneme is replaced by its phonetically similar partner in the same position and the result is a change of meaning. These pairs of words are called MINIMAL PAIRS and the pairs of phonemes are said to be CONTRASTIVE. /t/ and /d/ can be proved to be contrastive in this way, so they are separate phonemes:

pat – pad
town – down
latter – ladder

Clear and dark /l/ are not contrastive in RP (Received Pronunciation). You cannot replace one with the other in the same place in a word. Clear and dark /l/ are allophones of the same phoneme.

ALLOPHONES, then, are variants of the same phoneme. If we take /t/ we can consider the allophones it might have:

Allophone	*Position in the word*	*Example*
Dental	before /θ/ or /ð/	(eighth)
Post alveolar	before /r/	(tread)
Aspirated	before a vowel	(tea)
Unaspirated	after an /s/	(stay)
Nasal release	before /n/	(button)
Lateral release	before /l/	(bottle)
Non-audible		(football)
or	before other plosives	
No release		(wet day)

All these allophones are variations on the theme of /t/ and can make the sound of the phoneme change slightly. /t/ can also be made with the tip of the tongue curled back. This pronunciation is called retroflex and it is heard in the English of people whose principal language is of Indian origin.

If we consider that most other phonemes have at least two variants and some have many allophones, we may understand how important it is that the child should be presented with sounds in the context of words. The child often experiences difficulty in relating the sound he has learnt with the seemingly quite different sound he hears in words. What may seem like poor auditory discrimination could be that he hears only too well and is perceiving differences that we are able to ignore because we have a strong visual image. If we know the word is 'spell' or 'spin' and how it is spelt, then we are not likely to be sympathetic when he writes 'sbin' or 'sbell'. Yet that is what he is hearing!

Consider another example – the phoneme /l/. In the word 'lip' it is a clear /l/ made with the tip of the tongue touching the alveolar ridge and the air escaping laterally over the sides of the tongue. In the word 'calm' it is nasalized and swallowed up in the /m/ or not pronounced at all. In the word 'atlas' it is devoiced and so different again. In 'bottle' the back of the tongue is raised towards the velum giving a back vowel resonance. This dark /l/ creates particular difficulty and the child often tries to write in a vowel, for example 'schooel'. There is little about all these sounds that will tell a young child that he must use the same symbol for all. He does need individual help to guide him through these difficulties.

OVERLAPPING ARTICULATION AND NON-AUDIBLE RELEASE

If we take one example of this and look at the ending 'ct' in spelling, i.e. words like 'act', 'direct', 'perfect', etc., or the 'ct' used medially as in 'actor', we have a good example of a silent phoneme that we all know is there because we know how to *spell the word*.

In the word 'act' the tongue rises to an open front vowel position and the air passes freely over it /æ/. Then the back of the tongue rises to stop the air flow by touching the velum and forming a stop /k/. Before the back of the tongue drops to release the plosion of the /k/, the tip of the tongue has already formed another stop on the alveolar ridge for the /t/. Thus, the plosion of the /k/ is cut off by the onset of the

/t/ and, as the /k/ is voiceless, no sound escapes during the segment of time that we think we are saying it. There is a period of silence before the release of the /t/. We are asking a child, who may have a virtually non-existant visual memory, to listen to silence *and then write it*!

We do actually perceive a difference between 'act' and 'at' in that we pick up the tiny clue of the on-glide from /æ/ to /k/ as the tongue moves backwards and upwards. However, it is certain that many children do not, judging by the number of Schonell Spelling Tests one sees with the word 'direct' spelt 'diret'.

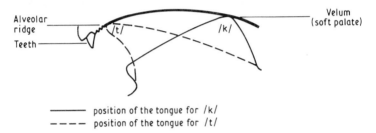

—————— position of the tongue for /k/
– – – – – position of the tongue for /t/

This effect can take place in rapid speech over word boundaries. 'Back door', for example, would have a silent /k/.

Other plosives can be affected in the same way. In the word 'utmost' the /t/ would be cut off by the closure of the lips for the /m/. It could, of course, be assimilated forward to the /p/ – /ʌpmǝʊst/, which would also be nasally released and mainly a period of silence.

The same 'silence' can occur when two phonemes are made in the same place of articulation and follow each other. 'Black cat' would be an example. The 'ck' at the end of 'black' would be held for an extra segment of time and not released separately before the 'c' of 'cat'. This double hold is extremely common in RP – 'white tie', 'thick cream', 'bad dog' – examples are legion!

'Aha!' we hear you say. 'I don't speak in such a sloppy way!' An effort at transcribing a taped recording of one's own speech may prove otherwise. But even if you do speak perfectly, the child will not necessarily do so when sub-vocalizing.

STRESS

In multisyllable words stress can change the sound of the vowel considerably. The unstressed vowel tends to sound like a schwa /ǝ/, leaving the writer unsure which vowel to use. Practice in phonemic transcription will bring this home to you.

If the word 'rebel' is used as a noun both vowels can sound like this:

/'rebʊl/ or /'rebḷ/.

If the same word is used as a verb the pronunciation can be:

/rɪ'bel/ or /rə'bel/.

Yet the spelling of all four pronunciations is 'rebel'.

Syllable stress can change with the grammatical use of the word although the spelling remains constant:

Noun/adjective		Verb	
/'æb strækt/	**ab**stract	/əb'strækt/	ab**stract**
/'fri: kwənt/	**fre**quent	/frɪ'kwent/	fre**quent**
/'æbsənt/	**ab**sent	/əb'sent/	ab**sent**
/'rekɔ:d/	**re**cord	/rə'kɔ:d/ or /rɪ'kɔ:d/	re**cord**

Although the spelling remains the same, a change of stress can give a word a totally different meaning, for example:

'The minute hand on my watch is minute.'
/ðə mɪnɪt hænd ɒn maɪ wɒtʃ ɪz maɪnju:t/
(or even 'The minute hand *om* my watch is minute'!).

Stress in words can change when the word is incorporated into a well-known phrase:

London**derry**	but	**Lond**onderry Air
Picca**dilly**	but	**Picc**adilly Circus
after**noon**	but	**af**ternoon tea
West**min**ster	but	**West**minster Abbey
prose**cu**tion	but	**prose**cution witness.

3   Teaching notes

There have been many structured programmes for remedial use published but the order in which they suggest concepts should be taught can vary. The following notes are set out under individual headings so that they may be more easily used in conjunction with any scheme of work.

GETTING STARTED

Children who fall behind their peers in learning to read and spell often lose confidence in themselves and then become so nervous of failure that they approach any extra help offered with a very negative attitude. It therefore seems sensible to try to get the child re-started in a relaxed and friendly way. Ideally one should try to work on a one-to-one basis, as in any group there are winners and losers and once again he may find himself doing less well than someone else. Competition can be brought in, but it should be competition against his own previous scores or times.

The usual situation is that the remedial teacher gets, at most, an hour a week alone with a child, but this time can be extended if the parents can be involved. The presence of parents during lessons is something many teachers would resist. However, if parents can sit in at a lesson and understand the way the work is proceeding, they are able to offer the child informed and constructive help with his revision exercises at home during the week. This increased reinforcement is invaluable. Parents are often accused of 'pushing' a child too far and this is, of course, a danger. One way of dealing with this is to put the whole question of homework into the hands of the child. He makes a pact with his therapist that he will give ten minutes a day to the work. He will choose the time when he thinks that he will feel most co-operative and he will set the kitchen pinger for a ten-minute session. When the ten minutes are up, the session will stop unless *he* passionately wants to finish something that is half done. Most parental help falls down at this point. If the child is co-operative and willing the parent thinks, 'While he is enthusiastic, I'll extend the session'. The child may soon find himself in the position of being forced to look reluctant in order to limit the time spent on the task and avoid getting overtired.

The presence of a parent during a lesson can be very helpful to relationships too. An anxious parent begins to relax considerably when she sees the teacher and child having a giggle about an error and the teacher quite unconcernedly re-presenting a fact that has already been learnt and forgotten several times already. It is this over-learning that is very necessary to this type of learning disabled child and a quiet acceptance of the fact that he needs to do it again yet another way eventually rubs off on the onlooker. The understanding of his difficulties that this observation gives most parents stands the child in good stead for the rest of his life.

Another area where parental involvement is of great benefit is in the relationship of parent and school. A parent who has become involved in a child's work and seen the degree of his difficulty will be less inclined to blame his teachers for his lack of achievement, realizing that if it is so difficult to teach him on a one-to-one basis, how impossible it would be in a class of thirty or so.

The child with perceptual learning difficulties needs help to make the link between the sound he makes with his organs of speech and the symbols that represent these sounds. He also needs to complete the circular process of turning these symbols back again into sounds in order to achieve any competence in reading and writing the majority of English words. The usual argument used for abandoning phonic teaching altogether is that this approach cannot be used for many English words and that phonics are no help at all when it comes to a word like 'enough'. The fact remains that there are some children who need a thorough, structured course in phonics if they are to learn at all. Words like 'enough' are in the minority, and if he is given the tools to deal with the more regular patterns he can use his energies on learning the irregular words as separate entities. Of course, it is a long and difficult process and the degree of the child's past failure produces a feeling of urgency and may lead teacher and parents to try to proceed too quickly so the child's brain may be flooded yet again with information he cannot assimilate. The teaching must be structural and gradual. If it can also be fun, then so much the better. That is the challenge of all remedial teaching. Teachers can vary the work by including visual patterns of words and look alike and kinaesthetic approaches like Fernauld tracing and letter case work. It is, of course, important that each small gain the child makes is appreciated and praised, because an important task for the remedial teacher is the restoration of the child's confidence in himself.

Although it is acknowledged that development of a child's free writing is essential in other aspects of his school work, for the purpose of restoring his confidence and teaching him to spell, dictation is invaluable. Short sentences using only those words which are within his spelling ability quickly rebuild his self respect. The mixture of joy and disbelief a child displays when he has written his first short paragraph with *no mistakes* can be very moving. Of course, these dictations must be very carefully prepared and must incorporate each new spelling concept as it is taught and also include revision work. As well as boosting his confidence these dictations can also increase the child's willingness to think sensibly about his mistakes. If a mistake is made and the child is convinced that the word would not have been included in the dictation if he had not already been given some instruction in its spelling pattern, he is more prepared to search his memory and produce a sensible alternative spelling. Wild irrelevant guesses become less frequent as lessons progress and the child becomes more conscientious as well as more confident.

If the teacher is to be of any real help to the child, however, she must understand the child's mistakes and appreciate the tiny perceptual clues by which we automatically learn to differentiate between similarly articulated sounds. The child with auditory perceptual difficulties will confuse phonemes with very slight auditory differences – the presence or absence of voice in similarly articulated phonemes, or the devoicing of phonemes that he has managed to learn in their more usual voiced form. He will confuse p/b, t/d, k/g, etc. The child with visual perceptual problems relies on his own phonetic spelling, and can be led astray by the sounds he makes in ordinary speech.

Every year, in phonetics classes, people begin by denying that they assimilate, elide, devoice, etc. It becomes a matter of considerable pride with some students and they insist that they do not use /tə/ instead of /tuː/, let alone the more extraordinary things like /reb buːts/ instead of 'red boots' and /ɔːwɪz/ instead of /ɔːlweɪz/.

Of course, not all a child's errors are made for phonetic reasons, but a surprising number are. A knowledge of phonetic pitfalls and traps will help the teacher to develop a sympathetic understanding of the pupil's difficulties. To have a teacher say, 'Yes, I can see why you wrote the word like that – we'll have to practise that sort of word and think about . . .', is a great relief and can help to cancel the feeling of failure the child experiences on having written 'jumpt' or 'diret' yet again.

PHONEMIC TRANSCRIPTION

Introspective listening to one's own speech can be very helpful in the understanding of a child's difficulties. A seemingly odd mistake can actually show the child's acute perception of the sounds he hears, coupled with a poor memory of what a word looks like. Alternatively, it could be that he has extremely poor auditory perception and lacks intuitive ability to differentiate between slightly different sounds.

There is no better way to train the ear than to practise phonemic transcription and we strongly recommend that teachers try to develop this skill. A short paragraph transcribed daily has been found to be the best method of learning the symbols, rather than sitting down and trying to memorize them *en bloc*. Revision of the vowel diphthong charts will be helpful too, as the symbols for these phonemes use the two elements of the vowel glide (see pp. 63–4). For instance /aɪ/ is a glide of the highest point of the tongue from an open front position to a closer front position, and the symbols used reflect that glide.

It is helpful, too, to read a short passage to a tape recorder and then try to record the actual phonemes heard. Initially you will find that you transcribe what you think you say, but after a time you will begin to realize that 'and' can be /ænd/ or a shorter form can be used /ənd/.

You could be using an even shorter form /ən/, or even /n̩/, in rapid colloquial speech.

You will realize that 'the' is pronounced /ði:/ before a vowel and /ðə/ before a consonant. You will begin to hear yourself assimilate and elide. This is the beginning of the sort of real listening we hope to develop.

Ordinary phonemic transcription is a broad recording of the sounds we make in speech and is enclosed in diagonal lines /æ/. No capital letters or punctuation are used as it is just the sounds that concern us. A pause is shown, however, by / and a full stop by //, thus:

/ju: wɪl faɪnd ðɪs dɪfɪkəlt tə ri:d/ əv kɔ:s//

You will find this difficult to read, of course.

The appearance of square brackets [] often puzzles students. These square brackets are used to show that a narrower transcription is being used showing greater phonetic detail. For instance allophonic variations would be shown in this way [ŋ] or [æ̃]. However, in ordinary transcription such detail is not necessary.

Progress in learning to transcribe is fairly rapid. Given a nursery rhyme to transcribe, a beginner might write:

//mɛəri: hæd eɪ lɪtl̩ læmb/
ɪts fli:s wɒs waɪt æs snəʊ//

This student is still thinking about each word individually and is also still tied up with spelling. However, some weeks later, the schwa has appeared and is being noticed. She has also realized that the final letter of 'lamb' is not pronounced and that the final sound of 'was' and 'as' is /z/. She has now become aware of the sounds of her own speech and might write:

//mɛərɪ hæd ə lɪtl̩ læm/
ɪts fli:s wəz waɪt əz snəʊ//

Another beginner transcribes:

//aɪv dʒʌst gɒt bæck frɒm ɪtæli://

Later, when assimilation and elision have been noticed, she realizes that she elides the final /t/ of 'just'. She notices that she assimilates the final /t/ of 'got' forward to a /p/ because of the influence of the following bilabial /b/. She also uses a schwa, clips short the final /ɪ/ in 'Italy' and has learnt that 'ck' is not necessary in phonemic transcription. The sound is /k/ and the symbol 'c' is not used at all because its sound is either /k/ or /s/ as in /kæt/ or /sɪtɪ/. Her new transcription would now read:

//aɪv dʒʌs gɒp bæk frəm ɪtəlɪ//

and she has reached a fairly sophisticated level of understanding of her own speech.

She will now be able to take more care when teaching individual sounds and be more sympathetic with the child whose visual skills are limited or slow to develop and who must refer back to the sound of words *every time he sits down to write*.

TEACHING INDIVIDUAL PHONEMES

Care should be taken to teach the alphabet sound/symbol relationships without adding a schwa to voiceless sounds, but if the child has learnt them in this way – /æ/, /bə/, /kə/, /də/, etc. – it is extremely unproductive to be too pernickety about it. It is better to allow him to continue to read the sounds from his flash cards in his way and then, when dictating them back to him (an important part of the exercise) to pronounce them correctly. If at first he does not recognize them, it will be necessary to repeat them twice, once with a schwa and once without. Quite often the correct pronunciation rubs off on him, and even if it does not he is hearing the phonemes as they usually sound within the word, which will enable him to recognize them. In any case, the individual sound/symbol relationships come at a very early stage of remediation and one would not wish to start a course of teaching with criticism and too much correction.

That schwa, of course, adds voicing (all vowels are voiced and /ə/ is a vowel) to otherwise voiceless phonemes and destroys other vital clues for the child. For instance /m/ is made with the lips closed and /n/ with them open. If you add /ə/ and make it /mə/ you lose this visual clue. The actual sounds produced for /m/ and /n/ are not very different on their own; we can *feel* the difference more readily than we can hear it. If you think of the oral cavity as a sound box, then only a slightly different resonance is audible. The air enters the mouth and reaches the barrier of the closed lips before escaping over the lowered soft palate via the nose for /m/. The air does not get as far for the /n/ because the passage is blocked by the tongue touching the alveolar ridge.

Some children are interested in an explanation of how a sound is made. They can be shown how there is more movement in a small piece of thin paper held before the lips when the sound is voiceless /p/, /t/ and /k/ and less movement when the sound is voiced /b/, /d/ and /g/. They can feel the vibration in their necks caused by the voicing, or hold their hands over their ears to hear the 'buzz'.

If the child has been taught to look at the letter, say the sound, listen to the sound and write the letter, his memory will often be triggered off by saying a sound out loud and feeling what his mouth is doing when he cannot think how to write a particular phoneme or morpheme.

There are many games and worksheets in existence for teaching the individual sounds. One interesting piece of equipment from the phonetics point of view is the Edith Norrie Lettercase.* This letter case is arranged phonetically. The first section contains sounds made with lips or lips and teeth, the second contains alveolar sounds and the third contains the back of the mouth sounds. Voiced sounds are represented by letters which are coloured green, voiceless are black and the vowels are red. The box also contains a small mirror for the child to see where he is making the sound. Some children really welcome being able to work out a difficult word with these letters before taking the final step and writing it. The actual kinaesthetic working out of changes and the visual reinforcement of them taking place helps too. For instance, to replace 'ck' on the word 'tack' and actually put down 'ke' to make it into 'take' seems to cement the ideas of short and long vowel differences.

The making of flash cards with a key picture on the back also seems to cement the sound for the child. If he thinks /d/ – 'dalek' or /c/ – 'cat', he is thinking of the sound both individually and within a word. One often hears children muttering these clue words and sounds to themselves and it is obviously of considerable help to some in making the sound/symbol relationship.

This applies even more when initial consonant blends are tackled. The blends alter the sounds considerably and frequently second and third elements are devoiced (see p. 16) or unaspirated (see p. 11). In these blends the provision of a key word helps to link the changed sound of the phonemes with the printed letters and /tr/ – 'train' or /st/

*Available from the Helen Arkell Dyslexia Centre, 14 Crondace Road, London SW6 4BB.

– 'star' unlocks the sound for him. Timed activities with the flashcards are useful for speeding up reading and card/picture matching games can be played. Filling in worksheets is not enough, and every activity should be matched with auditory reinforcement and as much multisensory back-up as possible.

THE CONSONANT DIGRAPHS 'sh', 'th' and 'ch'

These three digraphs need to be tackled fairly early in the teaching scheme. If you are trying to build success into the child's work with you and are restricting the work to phonemes already taught they can add considerably to the interest of the little sentences he can write.

'That dog is thin' could provide a useful lesson in the two sounds, voiced /ð/ and voiceless /θ/, that are represented by the letters 'th'. In most other phonemes, the voiced and voiceless sounds made in an identical place of articulation warrant two quite separate symbols. Perhaps this fact has been worrying the child and is causing some difficulty. On the other hand, perhaps he comes from a background where both these phonemes are usually represented by the sounds /f/ and /v/ – 'I fink I will go wiv you'.

'Sh' and 'ch'

These two digraphs are confusing. The visual similarity of the letters is not much help, so a lot of games, work sheets, sorting activities, etc. will be needed.

It sometimes helps to be able to point out that 'ch' has the tongue actually touching the alveolar ridge and is more plosive. In 'sh' the tongue does not touch the roof of the mouth and the sound is fricative. The visual clue of the finger raised to the lips sometimes helps with this one.

FINAL SOUNDS 'mp', 'nt', 'nk', /ŋk/ and 'nch'

These final blends of consonants are another difficult group for the child to perceive.

The nasals /m/, /n/ and /ŋ/ are not released orally. The velum lowers and allows the sound to escape nasally for a brief period, but the duration of the phoneme is shortened by the following voiceless sound, so the child tends to ignore the nasal altogether. It is quite helpful to ask the child to repeat words with and without the nasal to demonstrate the difference, i.e. 'I'll say "clap" and "clamp" and you repeat it and see if you can hear and feel the buzz in your nose'.

/ŋk/

This sound is particularly awkward. One has usually spent time teaching 'ing' and 'ang', 'eng', 'ong', 'ung'. 'Nk' sounds like /ŋk/ and it is often written as 'ngk' by the child. We assimilate the /n/ back to /ŋ/ because of the following velar phoneme /k/. He may have to be specifically taught that when he hears /ŋk/ he writes 'nk'.

/ns/ *and* /nts/

Few English RP speakers retain the distinction between words ending with these two blends:

> mints – mince
> tents – tense
> plants – dance
> assistants – assistance

the sound /nts/ being used in all cases. Perhaps an explanation of the plural use of 'ts' would help here.

Plurals

The teacher needs to point out to some children that sometimes /s/ will sound like /z/ when one is making plurals. If the preceding consonant or vowel is voiced the plural *sound* will be /z/, as in /dɒgz/. If the preceding sound is voiceless, on the other hand, the plural will sound like /s/ as in /kæts/. Of course, the teacher needs to be able to hear this herself!

PAST TENSES

The *regular* past tense 'ed' has three distinct sounds.

After a voiceless phoneme it sounds like /t/.

hopped

After a voiced phoneme it sounds like /d/.

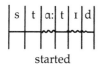

robbed

After /t/ or /d/ it sounds like /ɪd/.

| s | t | ɑː | t | ɪ | d |

started

The final cluster 'mped' as in 'jumped' is further complicated by the fact that the /p/ is realized as a period of silence. (See pp. 25–6.)

The child can fill in sounds in the brackets on a work sheet and it can be stressed that whatever he *hears*, he *writes* 'ed'.

hopped	(t)
jumped	(t)
telephoned	(d)
started	(id)
cracked	(t)
robbed	(d)
waited	(id) or even (ed).

Irregular verbs like 'sent' have another set of rules and can be tackled at a later stage. The 'ed' suffix can be revised and the fact that it is added to a whole word (hop + ed = hopped, jump + ed = jumped) pointed out. In 'sent' etc., if the /t/ sound is removed one is not left with a word at all.

SHORT AND LONG VOWEL SOUNDS

Before any progress can be made with concepts like Magic e, doubling consonants after a short vowel and the many spelling patterns that rely on vowel sounds, it is necessary that the child should have a thorough knowledge of the sounds of short and long vowels. He can be taught to mark short vowels with breves (căt) and long vowels with macrons (mē). If he is quite young he will enjoy little logos of Mr Short Vowel and Mr Long Vowel. He may feel too old for such nonsense, of course, but still enjoy being told how you teach it to the younger children!

If reference is made to the chart on page 63, it will be seen from the very close proximity of certain vowels that the child with perception problems will have great difficulty discriminating between them. /ɪ/ and /e/ are very easily confused. /æ/ and /ʌ/ are another pair which cause trouble. It seems best to teach a front vowel first. /ɪ/ is a good choice as quite a few simple words can be made with it and small sentences can be invented to give a feeling of progress into real writing. This should be followed by /ɒ/ perhaps, leaving /e/ until much later.

There are many worksheets and games on the market that can be used for teaching these basic and necessary sounds. Board games can be played with vowel sounds, or cartoons of Mum and Dad can be thumped when the sound /ʌ/ and /æ/ are heard. Bill and Ben can also be thumped for /ɪ/ and /e/ and a great deal of fun can be had by all, especially if the teacher has a cartoon of the child to thump if he gets it wrong! This game is a good tension reliever too.

Children with perceptual problems do experience difficulty and work spent on teaching them at an early stage is very helpful later on. Constant revision is needed to keep the correct sounds and a short period of each lesson should be devoted to vowels for some time.

PROBLEMS WITH /r/

The first difficulty we meet with /r/ is its name. The child tries to use it for the sound /ɑː/. It should certainly be taught with just the sound /r/ and no added schwa. Repeated reminders that 'r' just makes the sound /r/ should be given and that to get the sound /ɑː/ you need 'ar' (unless it comes before 's', 'f', 'th', etc. in the South of England, in which case just 'a' will do). Another problem is the devoiced fricative /r/ in tr and str, as mentioned in *voicing* on p. 17.

Then we have the vowel sounds /ɑː/, /ɔː/ and /ɜː/ which use 'r' as the second component – 'ar', 'or' and 'er'. Although the letter 'r' is used it is not pronounced as /r/ in RP. Flashcards can be helpful, with games saying words and pointing to the right card.

Intrusive /r/

We may insert an /r/ sound in rapid speech when one is not present in the spelling of a word. This intrusive /r/ often appears, therefore, in the child's writing. /lɔːr ənd ɔːdə/ – 'law and order', /ʃɑːr əv pɜːʃə/ – 'Shah of Persia', are two favourite examples.

Linking /r/

When linking /r/ appears it does not create so much difficulty because it *is* present in the spelling. It appears before a vowel but not before a consonant. /fɔːr æplz/ – 'four apples', but /fɔː bəʊts/ – 'four boats'.

/dʒɔːr əʊpn̩ waɪd/ – 'jaw open wide' = Intrusive /r/
/dɔːr əʊpn̩ waɪd/ – 'door open wide' = Linking /r/

The child who is being taught about long vowels also gets into difficulties with /r/. In words like 'care' the /r/ changes the sound of the long ā from /eɪ/ to /ɛə/. Similarly in 'fire' the sound is changed from /aɪ/ to /aɪə/. How very confusing for the child who is being taught about Magic e. The child has learnt that in Magic e words the sound is consonant – long vowel – consonant and that the final 'e' just sits there silently doing its job, i.e. making the vowel long. Yet here is a word where the final sound is one long vowel glide and the consonant /r/ is not pronounced at all in RP although West Country people would do so and so would Americans. It is advisable to separate these words from the group and teach them as a separate entity.

/r/ really is an awkward phoneme. Its very manner of articulation adds to its difficulty. The child does not get the kinaesthetic feel of the sound in the mouth easily as it is vowel-like in the way it is made. The rolled /r/ or the flap (like Noel Coward) also appear from time to time in different accents. The flap is made by the tongue tip actually touching the alveolar ridge very rapidly indeed so, in effect, it is an extremely rapid /d/.

The child may have difficulty in articulating the /r/ as it requires considerable rigidity of the tongue muscles and many children with learning difficulties also have speech difficulties.

This awkward little phoneme causes quite a lot of problems.

1 The sound /j/ is used at the beginning of words like 'yacht' and 'yes' as a consonant, but it is made as a vocalic glide to the following vowel, so to the child it does not have quite the feel of a consonant.
2 When /j/ follows a voiceless fortis consonant it is made in a voiceless fricative manner. Words like 'cube' will have this different sounding phoneme intruding before the vowel sound, i.e. /kju:b/, whereas words like 'rude' have a simple /u:/ sound. These two entirely different versions of ū can be spelt identically:

/u:/	/ju:/
blew	new
chew	few
crew	dew
flew	stew
	view (In this word 'i' seems to take its place)
	knew

This can cause confusions so it is worth while splitting these two groups and teaching them as separate items, pointing out to the child that the spelling 'ew' can have two sounds.

Further complications arise with the word 'queue'. Having been taught that the sound of 'qu' is /kw/ (and so it is generally) here is a word where the sound is [k̥j] and a rather fricative [j] at that. The phonetic symbol for this sound is [ç] and it is a voiceless palatal fricative not usually used in English at all except in these circumstances. Following /p/, /t/, /k/ and /h/ and before /u:/, /ʊ/, /ə/ this [ç] will be found causing all sorts of confusion as the child tries to write it! Words using this sound are 'pew' /pju:/, 'tune' /tju:n/, 'cube' /kju:b/, 'huge' /hju:dʒ/, and 'curious' /kjʊərɪəs/.

3 Following 'sp', 'st' and 'sk' an ordinary /j/ will be used, but it will be slightly devoiced, i.e. 'spurious', 'stew' and 'askew' /spju:rɪəs/, /stju:/, /əskju:/.

To complicate matters still further the *letter* 'y' (the alphabet symbol for the sound /j/) sometimes represents a vowel both within and at the end of words, for example 'mummy', 'my', 'cycle'. In these words 'y' is used for the vowel sounds /i:/, /aɪ/ and /aɪ/. We also find /ɪ/ as in 'cygnet'.

SYLLABLE DIVISION

One of the most useful methods of breaking down a child's fear of 'long words' is syllable division. At first glance this seems to be very complicated and well beyond the capabilities of most children who need remedial work. However, it is invaluable in the teaching of both reading and writing and a great stimulus to the older child who needs a more academic approach.

It is fairly easy to build syllable division into the structure of a phonic programme to a greater or lesser degree, depending upon the age and IQ of the child and many of our children enjoy and absorb it if it is introduced carefully and gradually. An older child, for example, can be taught about DIPHTHONG syllables and the younger child can call them FRIEND SYLLABLES. If syllable division is introduced at each stage of language development the whole subject need not be onerous.

We have found that quite small children enjoy breaking up words into 'beats'. A few simple rules need to be mentioned. If two consonants appear between two vowels, you divide between them – 'hop/ping' – unless, of course, they make one sound like 'th'. The child can beat out words on the desk – two bangs for 'pa/per', one bang for 'desk'. Words can be written on strips of paper and cut up with scissors, mixed up and sorted out again. He can be taught to try words two ways.

hū/man ✓
hŭm/an ✗

The work can start quite early with the marking of short and long vowel sounds:

sō sŏb
bē bĕt.

This demonstrates that an open syllable has the vowel on the end and that vowel will be long. A final consonant closes the syllable and shortens the vowel.

Already he has learnt about two types of English syllable!

As he progresses to words containing 'ar', 'or' and 'er' (we would leave 'ir' and 'ur' until much later) he meets his third type – the vowel + r syllable sometimes referred to as R-COMBINATION or VR syllable, and he can divide words like

ar/tist

and (when he has learnt that /i:/ on the end of a word is spelt 'y')

ar/my.

He can begin to mark the 'beats': o – open, c – closed and vr – VOWEL + R. The next type he is likely to meet is the dreaded Magic e. As he learns about this concept he can be introduced to:

bē/cāme rē/fūse

and slowly over a period of months he has built up to four types of syllable. Each time a new one is added he will need revision as he will have forgotten the exact details, and this all strengthens his ability to break down words into manageable 'chunks'. The delight of a small child who realizes that he can write

o c vr c o   c   c   c
u/niv/er/sit/y and mack/in/tosh

when he thought he could only manage 'one beat' words is a joy to see.

The next type to be tackled is the DIPHTHONG or DIGRAPH. These are often called FRIEND SYLLABLES and contain two vowels. The final type is the SYLLABIC L. The rule with this latter is 'count back three from the 'e', thus:

băt/tle trī/fle.

This rule is a great help with the problem of whether to double the consonant before the 'le'.

As so many months – or even years – elapse between the addition of each new type, it is worth having a check list in some reference book (perhaps he has a rule book) and adding each new syllable as he meets it, for example:

Open – o – bē sō wē mȳ
Closed – c – bĕt sŏb wĕt

V + r – vr – far for her
Magic e – e – cāme hōme hūge
Diphthong/
    digraph — d – road train seem
Syllabic l – l – bằttle trĩfle bồttle ằpple

The child can also be encouraged to break words down into root words, prefixes and suffixes. Older children will then meet interesting facts when looking at Latin prefixes, for instance. Some prefixes do not always appear as they have been learnt, and having read the section on assimilation we can now understand why! For example:

ad + pear = appear
ad + rest = arrest
ad + prove = approve
con + pose = compose
con + plain = complain
dis + vide = divide
in + mense = immense
in + rigate = irrigate
sub + ply = supply
sub + port = support

Simple rules for suffixing as found in Rak's *Spellbound* and *Spell of Words* and Hornsby and Shear's *Alpha to Omega* can then clear up a great many spelling difficulties for the older child. (See *suggestions for further reading*, pp. 66–7.)

Particular attention can be given to stress (see pp. 26–7).

Suffixing after a stressed syllable

Games can be played beating out stress in words and changing the stress to change the meaning:

'rebel re'bel.

If a child experiences difficulty in hearing stress, it sometimes helps to say the word with the wrong stress:

'forget for'get.

A useful spelling rule can then be introduced. If the word is a ba**boom** word, (i.e. the stress is on the last syllable) then you double the final consonant before a vowel suffix:

ad**mit**	ad**mitt**ed	ad**mitt**ing	ad**mitt**ance
for**get**	for**gott**en	for**gett**ing.	

This rule does not apply to words ending in 'l'. Always double the 'l' regardless of stress.

You can see this rule working when the stress changes with the addition of a particular suffix.

pre**fer**	pre**ferr**ed	pre**ferr**ing
but	**pref**erence	**pref**erable

The child can also be made aware of the fact that the addition of a suffix often changes the stress given to the root word elements resulting in a distortion of vowels in unstressed syllables. He can be encouraged to analyse the structure of the word and refer back to the root for a clearer indication of the original vowel.

USING SPELLING ERRORS FOR GUIDANCE

Children come to the remedial teacher at various stages in their learning process, and she has to decide on a teaching programme for them. A useful way to approach the problem is to dictate a few words from the early stages of language build up and observe the errors the child makes. It is wise to pick the more unusual words from the various strings in order to avoid those of which he might have a vague sight memory and to discover whether he is really using phonic skills. For example he might know the word 'bell' and double the final 'l' but the word 'smell' would be less likely to be lurking in his sight memory and would carry the added bonus of conveying whether he can deal with the initial blend 'sm'.

Diagnosis from spelling errors can give a lot of information and be of enormous help in planning a teaching programme. The child may be dealing competently with the earlier structures, having been well taught up to a certain level. He may read and write cvc words and use consonant blends fairly well but perhaps in his writing he has used the word 'sandwich' and written 'samwig'. This one mistake conveys a wealth of information and suggestions for future work.

1 He would benefit by work breaking down syllables and stressing enunciation. He has fallen into the phonetic trap of hearing the assimilation of 'nd' forward to an /m/. Perhaps he would be interested in the story of the origins of this word.

2 His use of 'g' shows poor enunciation and also lack of phonic knowledge. If the sound he was aiming for was /dʒ/ then he should be taught that 'g' only sounds like /dʒ/ when it is followed by 'e', 'i' or 'y'.

This one spelling mistake leads to many weeks of useful work. To tackle the 'dge' or 'ge' ending, one needs to revise short and long vowel sounds. Then work through 'soft g' word initially, medially and finally. After this is well absorbed and another revision of short and long vowel sounds has been undertaken then, and only then, is one ready to tackle 'dge' after a short vowel sound as in 'badge, hedge, bridge, lodge and trudge'. One could follow with the 'tch' rule and then point out that 'sandwich' is one of the few exceptions to this rule, like 'such', 'much', 'rich', 'which', 'ostrich', etc. All this will give many weeks of work, revision and a point of beginning for this particular child.

Another child is at a much earlier stage of work and writes 'ask' as 'rsg'. Again he may well be hearing 'sg', as the difference between /k/ and /g/ will be neutralized in this position (see p. 11). He needs to be told that 'sg' is not used in English because it sounds the same as 'sk'. He also needs a lesson on the fact that 'r' only makes the sound /r/ and not /a:/. One should go right back to the names and sounds of the letters of the alphabet, sorting out for him the difference between the name and the sound in depth. More lessons are needed on the fact that /a:/ is usually written 'ar', but that in the south of England at least 'a' alone can sound like /a:/ before 's', 'f' and 'th' as in 'last', 'after' and 'bath'. If he lives in a part of the country where most people say /bæθ/ then perhaps this latter section could be omitted, depending on his degree of difficulty and intelligence.

Further examples of diagnosis from spelling errors are:

took = tuk	Well, the sound /ʊ/ *is* written 'u' in 'pull', 'full', etc. The child needs to learn 'book', 'cook', 'look', 'took', etc. as a separate group.
direct = diret	The 'c' *is* silent (see *overlapping articulation* on pp. 25–6).
admit = abmit	The 'd' is assimilated forward to a 'b' very often in everyday speech.
dog = dok	The informed teacher will think about voicing and place of articulation and will not be

surprised when a child always writes 'dok' instead of 'dog', 'pat' instead of 'pad', or 'cap' instead of 'cab'. This teacher will make a note:
(a) to do some work on discrimination of voiced/voiceless phonemes. Perhaps she will use exercises employing the knowledge that /k/ would shorten the duration of the vowel (see pp. 7–8)
(b) she would realize that in the word 'dog'

the /g/ is partially devoiced and can sound like /k/ if you have no memory of how the word *looks*. The child may need this final sound stressed with much added voicing of the /g/
(c) she would note that *at some future date but not now* this child needs to learn the rule that the short vowels ă, ĕ, ĭ, ŏ, ŭ need help and that we double 'l', 's' and 'f' after them. As we cannot double 'k' in English, we use 'ck'. This child could benefit by some work on ăck, ĕck, ĭck, ŏck and ŭck.

spring = sbring   If a child confuses p/b, it is easy to look at the symbols for those sounds and decide that he is rotating the letters. This is something that learning disabled children frequently do and it would be a reasonable assumption. However, a knowledge of voicing and place of articulation might make one think again about his perception of the voicing of the /b/. Perhaps he is rotating or perhaps he genuinely hears the /p/ and /b/ as the same sound. In fact, in the consonant blends 'sp' and 'spr', he does hear the same sound – we are the ones who know that one never writes 'sb' or 'sbr'. He needs to be told!

last = lrs   The letter 'r' is called /a:/, so the sound /a:/ might be written 'r' with any luck. He needs work on the difference between sounds and names of letters. The final 't' in this word is often elided, i.e. /lɑ:s naɪt/.

It will be seen that spelling errors can be caused by both lack of phonic knowledge and the traps that the child can be led into by the way we speak.

WORDS OF WARNING

1 Never presume that the child remembers *anything* just because he has been taught it in the past. Before starting on any new 'rule' think back and make a list of the things he may need to revise. For example to teach 'ge/dge' word finally, he needs to remember that an 'e' on the end of a vowel/consonant/vowel pattern will lengthen the first vowel (Magic e). He may even need to revise the long and short vowel sounds. He also needs to remember that 'g' sounds like /dʒ/ when followed by an 'e'. Thus in the word 'hedge', the 'e' is necessary to make the /dʒ/ sound and then the 'd' must be inserted to keep the first vowel short. Phonetically 'd' is acceptable here because the tongue goes to the alveolar ridge before dropping to /ʒ/ to make the /dʒ/ sound. He may like to have all this explained to him or he may prefer a simple 'rule' – after a short vowel use 'dge'.

2 All reading activities should be repeated with the child writing the sound he hears, to ensure that he can also spell. Many worksheets given to children as spelling exercises are, in fact, simply exercises in reading and copying.

3 If worksheets or computer 'games' are given to the child for unsupervised working, take care that the exercise is really teaching him the complete concept. It is very easy to devise careful work plans and assume the child will be as conscientious as the compiler and will seek out all the knowledge the package offers. In practice, he might well simply run down the worksheet dutifully filling all spaces with the required vowel digraph *without ever reading the word he is completing*.

Computer games can easily become simply visual exercises of shape manipulation and the child might never read or put sounds to the patterns of letters he is learning to copy. If he does and has been taught to look for phonic patterns he may be very confused by the mixture of sounds represented by some visually similar patterns. Consider a simple word list: gas, has, ask, was, ash. In each case the grouping of 'as' represents different sound combinations. In the early stages of phonic work he may well not be able to cope with this approach and it would be safer to restrict word strings to patterns that are phonetically similar as well as visually similar so that the auditory pattern is linked with the visual pattern.

4 The phonemes of English

Ordinary speech is made on breath which travels from the lungs, through the throat and is expelled through the mouth or nose. There are various clicks and ejective phonemes (individual sounds) which are made using air that has built up and been held on the way through the throat or oral cavity, or which use ingressive air, but generally speaking the airstream is outward flowing. On its way it is modified in various ways.

The first place of modification is the vocal folds. These are two elastic folds of muscle extending across the larynx. They can vibrate rapidly adding 'voice' to a phoneme, or they can remain open and relaxed producing a 'voiceless' phoneme. We can also close them and 'hold our breath', of course, and they can be narrowed and tensed to produce a whisper. A voiceless phoneme is made with more air force and described as FORTIS while a voiced phoneme has less force and is termed LENIS. When voiced phonemes are devoiced by their situation within the word, or the effect of other phonemes around them, it is often this force, or the lack of it, that helps us distinguish between the voiced and voiceless pairs, e.g. p/b, t/d, k/g.

A phoneme is further modified by the placement of the velum (soft palate), the tongue and the lips.

The organs of articulation

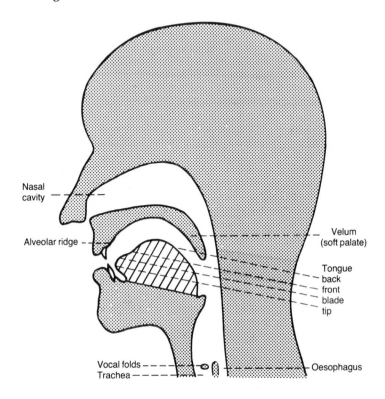

Nasal cavity

Alveolar ridge

Velum (soft palate)

Tongue
back
front
blade
tip

Vocal folds
Trachea

Oesophagus

THE PLOSIVES

If we study the order in which a child acquires speech, we will see that the plosives are achieved fairly early. He soon learns to produce nice, juicy, plopping sounds with his lips and make /p/ and /b/.

The velum (soft palate) must be raised to shut off the nasal resonator so that the air has to pass out through the mouth, where the placement of the lips or the tongue provides a barrier. The air builds up behind this closure or stop and then escapes with force (PLOSION) when it is released.

Voiceless and voiced bilabial plosives /p/ and /b/

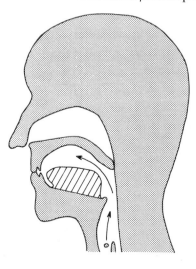

1 Vocal folds: /p/ open, /b/ vibrating.
2 Velum raised.
3 Tongue relaxed, or moving in anticipation of next sound. (For example, in the word 'hopeless' the tongue would be rising to the alveolar ridge for the following /l/ during the closure of the lips for the /p/.)
4 Lips closed initially. Air escapes with force when closure released. Shape affected by surrounding phonemes (say 'pea' and 'pot').

Voiceless and voiced alveolar plosives /t/ and /d/

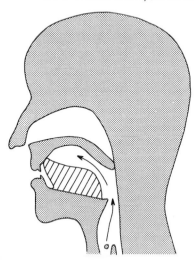

1 Vocal folds: /t/ open, /d/ vibrating.
2 Velum raised.
3 Tongue: tip raised to touch alveolar ridge and rims contacting upper side teeth. Released with plosion.
4 Lips open and shape conditioned by adjacent sounds (try saying 'too' and 'tea').

Voiceless and voiced velar plosives /k/ and /g/

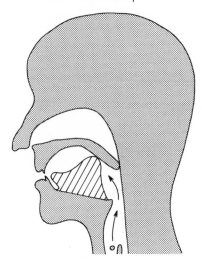

1 Vocal folds: /k/ open, /g/ vibrating.
2 Velum raised.
3 Tongue: back of tongue raised to touch soft palate initially and released with plosion.
4 Lips: open. Shape conditioned by adjacent phonemes (try saying 'car' and 'key').

Glottal plosive

RP speakers use a glottal stop more than they like to admit. The vocal folds close and air builds up below them to be released suddenly when they part. It is often used as a syllable boundary marker between two vowels [dʒɪʔɒmətrɪ] – 'geometry' or to stress the fact that the person is not using intrusive /r/ [lɔː ʔənd ɔːdə] – 'law and order'. It is also used to stress a word or a vowel [ʔenɪwʌn] – 'Has *any*one seen it?' There are a great many other uses of this particular phoneme, quite apart from the traditional Cockney [bʌʔə] – 'butter' etc.

THE FRICATIVES

In this group of phonemes the sound is produced by two organs of speech being brought close together and the channel narrowed enough for friction to be produced. This friction may or may not be accompanied by voice.

One can make bilabial fricatives, but we do not use them in English. There are symbols for them in the phonetic alphabet and you can try to make them by blowing voicelessly through nearly closed lips as you would to blow out a candle, and then blowing with added voice. We do, however, make and use a labio-dental fricative pair /f/ and /v/.

Voiceless and voiced labio-dental fricatives /f/ and /v/

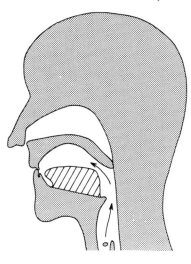

1 Vocal folds: /f/ open, /v/ vibrating.
2 Velum raised.
3 The tongue may be moving in anticipation of an adjacent vowel.
4 The lower lip makes light contact with the upper teeth, so that the air passes through with friction. The shape of the lips varies (try saying 'fe, fo, fi, fum').

Voiceless and voiced dental fricatives /θ/ and /ð/

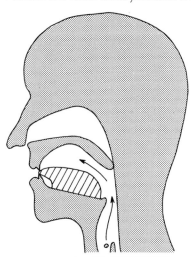

1 Vocal folds: /θ/ open, /ð/ vibrating.
2 Velum raised.
3 The rims of the tongue make contact with the upper side teeth, and the tip makes light contact with the upper incisors so that the air escaping causes friction.
4 The lip spread will depend on adjacent phonemes (try saying 'thee' and 'though').

Voiceless and voiced alveolar fricatives /s/ and /z/

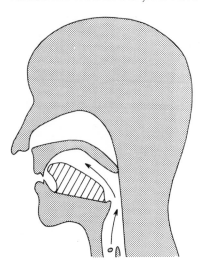

1 Vocal folds: /s/ open, /z/ vibrating.
2 Velum raised.
3 The rims of the tongue make contact with the upper side teeth and the tip and blade of the tongue make light contact with the upper alveolar ridge, allowing the air to pass over the tongue and through the gap with friction. Some people lower the tip to contact the lower front teeth and the friction is produced between the blade of the tongue and the alveolar ridge.
4 The lip position will depend on the adjacent phonemes (try saying 'see' and 'so').

Voiceless and voiced palato-alveolar fricatives /ʃ/ and /ʒ/

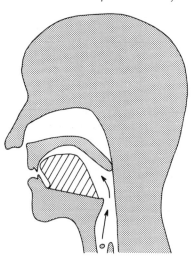

1 Vocal folds: /ʃ/ open, /ʒ/ vibrating.
2 Velum raised.
3 The side rims of the tongue contact the upper side teeth. The tip, blade and front of the tongue are raised. The tip and front make light contact with the alveolar ridge and the blade is raised towards the hard palate.
4 Some speakers use lip rounding, while others vary the lip shape.

Glottal fricative (voiceless /h/)

/h/ is made by a strong, voiceless airstream through the vocal folds, which are beginning to tighten up for the onset of the vibration for the vowel which always follows. There is a voiced variant which is sometimes used to stress the /h/ between vowels as in 'perhaps' /pəhæps/ and on the stage in order to amuse. ('A handbag?')

AFFRICATES

Palato-alveolar affricates /tʃ/ and /dʒ/

Stop stage of /tʃ/ and /dʒ/

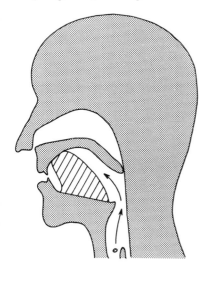

1 Vocal folds: /tʃ/ open, /dʒ/ vibrating.
2 Velum raised.
3 The tip, blade and rims of the tongue connect initially with the alveolar ridge and side teeth, forming a stop. The front of the tongue is raised towards the hard palate in readiness for the second element, which is fricative. A slow fricative release is made with the air escaping over the surface of the tongue with friction occurring between the blade and front of the tongue and the alveolar-palatal section of the roof of the mouth.
4 The lips are open and the shape determined by the following phoneme.

THE NASALS

The three nasal phonemes that we use are /n/, /m/ and /ŋ/. Nasal consonants are made in much the same way as plosives but with one major difference. The velum is lowered, allowing an escape of air into the nasal cavity and on outwards through the nose. They are usually voiced, although a somewhat devoiced variant may be heard if they are preceded by a voiceless consonant, e.g. /sm/, /sn/, /tm/, etc. as in /sməʊk/, /sneɪk/, /ʌtməʊst/ – 'smoke', 'snake' and 'utmost'.

Bilabial nasal /m/

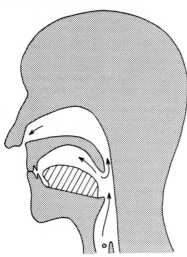

1 Vocal folds vibrating.
2 Velum lowered.
3 Tongue relaxed, or anticipating position of adjacent vowel etc.
4 Lips closed. Shape affected by surrounding phonemes (say 'my' and 'move').

Alveolar nasal /n/

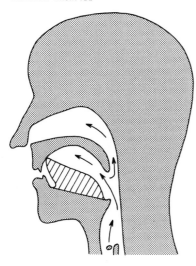

1 Vocal folds vibrating.
2 Velum lowered.
3 Tongue forming closure with alveolar ridge and upper teeth as in /t/, /d/. The tongue remains in position, though, and air escapes through nasal cavity.
4 Lips parted. Shape affected by surrounding phonemes (say 'knee' and 'no').

Velar Nasal /ŋ/ *spelt 'ng'*

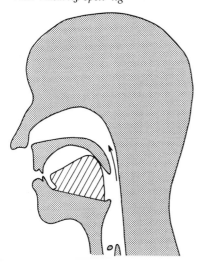

1 Vocal folds vibrating.
2 Velum lowered.
3 Tongue back raised to form a closure with velum. The point of closure will vary slightly, the contact being more advanced for words with preceding front vowel and more retracted for words with preceding back vowel (say 'thing' and 'song').
4 Lips parted. Shape affected by preceding vowel.

A less common partly devoiced allophone of /ŋ/ can be heard when the syllabic /ŋ̩/ is used, i.e. the word 'bacon' /beɪkŋ̩/. Another common London pronunciation of /ŋ/ is /ŋk/, i.e. the word 'something' pronounced /sʌmfɪŋk/ and another less popular pronunciation is /n/ as in 'huntin', shootin' and fishin''.

The auditory differences in the three nasal sounds /m/, /n/ and /ŋ/ are caused by the relative size of the oral chamber, the different resonances created and the acoustic effect of the movements of the speech organs to and from the place of articulation. In /m/ the air goes right forward into the mouth before being expelled through the nose. In /n/ the oral cavity is smaller because of the position of the tongue and in /ŋ/ the air cannot enter the oral cavity because of the closure formed by the back of the tongue being in contact with the velum. This auditory difference is very slight indeed.

LATERALS

These sounds are all allophones (variations) of the alveolar lateral phoneme /l/ but it is not commonly appreciated how different the three main allophones sound. The lateral is made by a partial closure of the oral cavity by the tongue tip articulating with the alveolar ridge. The rims of the tongue, however, are lowered to allow the air to escape laterally. It is difficult to feel this passage of warm lung air, but if one makes the sound /l/ while breathing in, it is easier to feel the cold external air passing over the sides of the tongue.

We use clear /l/ before vowels as in 'log' /lɒg/, and /j/ as in 'million' /mɪljən/.

We use a voiceless allophone following /p/ as in 'plan' /plæn/, and /k/ as in 'clean' /kli:n/.

Dark /l/ is used after a vowel at the end of a word – 'fill' /fɪl/, 'ball' /bɔːl/; after a vowel and before a consonant – 'help' /help/, 'bills' /bɪlz/; and as a syllabic sound following a consonant – 'little' /lɪtl̩/, 'bridle' /braɪdl̩/.

Alveolar lateral

Clear /l/

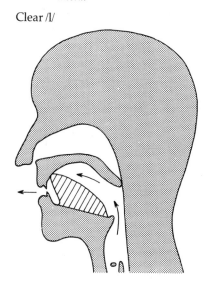

1 Vocal folds vibrating.
2 Velum raised.
3 Tongue tip touching
   centre of alveolar ridge
   with rims lowered to
   allow air to escape
   laterally. Front of
   tongue somewhat raised
   too.
4 Lips influenced by
   adjacent vowel (say
   'lead' and 'load').

Dark /l/

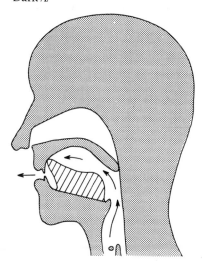

As above but:
3 Tongue tip touching
   centre of alveolar ridge
   with rims lowered. The
   front of the tongue is
   slightly depressed and
   the back raised to a back
   vowel (or velarized)
   position (say 'ball' or
   'school').

POST ALVEOLAR FRICTIONLESS CONTINUANT /r/

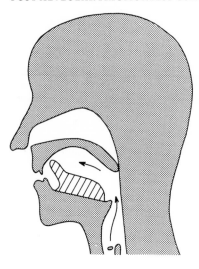

1 Vocal folds vibrating.
2 Velum raised.
3 Tongue tip raised towards rear part of alveolar ridge but not touching it. There is a spoon shaped depression in the upper surface and the back rims touch the side teeth.
4 The lip shape is largely determined by the following vowel, i.e. spread for a front vowel and rounded for a back vowel (say 'read' and 'rod').

There are many variants of this phoneme. When it occurs in the blends /tr/ and /dr/ it is realized so quickly that the tongue does not have time to lower quite as far as usual and so the /r/ is fricative. In the blend /tr/ it is also devoiced. The sound is so different from the /tərə/ taught in some classes.

Another fun variant is the 'Cabinet Minister's /r/'. This allophone is made by raising the bottom lip and creating a labio-dental (but without friction) by articulating with the upper front teeth. Watching for this labio-dental can even make Party Political Broadcasts quite riveting to watch on TV!

There is, too, the 'flap' where the tongue actually touches the alveolar ridge momentarily (listen to Noel Coward) and the rolled /r/.

VOWELS

The vowel is a less precise phoneme to describe. If you imagine the oral cavity as a sounding chamber with the tongue rising and falling to alter the shape of that chamber, you will realize that the precise position of the tongue will have to vary from person to person to produce the same sound because the shape of the oral cavity will be variable. Some people have broad cavities and some narrow, depending upon the shape of their heads. The perception of a vowel, then, can only be of an acoustic nature.

The phonetician, Daniel Jones, worked out a system of describing vowels by making a chart of the most extreme positions of the tongue during vowel production. The sounds made at the extreme positions numbered 1–8 on our diagram are called Cardinal Vowels and each has its symbol. Their study is not relevant to the teaching of spelling, but they do act as useful reference points in the study of the vowels we use in English.

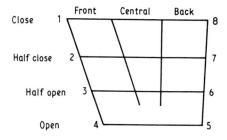

Imagine this chart implanted in the oral cavity and remember that the position of the highest part of the tongue will determine the sound of the vowel.

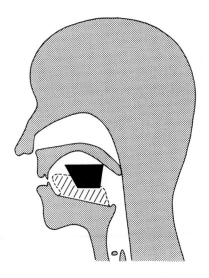

Thus, the highest and most forward position in which a vowel sound can be made is called Cardinal Vowel 1. We would describe it as a close, front vowel and know that the highest point of the tongue would be in a position corresponding to the top left hand corner of the chart. The nearest vowel to this point that English speakers use is /iː/ as in 'fee'. This vowel /iː/ is made with the tongue front raised to a height slightly below and behind the extreme front close position. The lips are spread, the tongue tense and the side rims contact the upper molars.

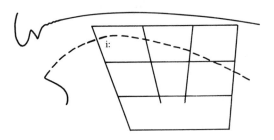

If you take several students in a group and ask them all to say 'tea' the actual location of the /iː/ will vary because they all have slightly different backgrounds and speech patterns.

The nearest vowel to Cardinal Vowel 5 that English speakers use is /ɑː/ as in 'car'. When making this vowel /ɑː/ the *back* of the tongue is the highest point and it will be in a back open position with the lips in a more rounded shape.

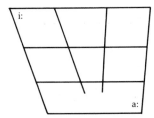

Monophthongs in RP

The monophthongs are:
i: feet
ɪ pit
e red
æ bat
ʌ bun
ɜ: bird
ə paper
ɑ: hard
ɒ hot
ɔ: lord
ʊ good
u: food

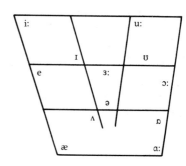

Diphthongs in RP

Here the highest point of the tongue glides from one vowel to another.

Closing diphthongs

eɪ date
aɪ time
əʊ boat
aʊ cow
ɔɪ coin

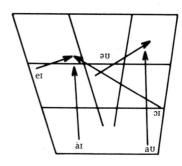

The second element of the vowel glide is closer to the palate, hence the term 'closing'.

Centring diphthongs

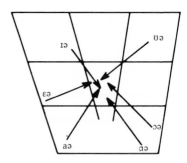

ɪə dear
ɛə care
ʊə pure
aɪə fire (aə)
aʊə power (aə)
ɔə sore (some pronunciations)

Triphthongs

The pronunciation of all these vowel glides varies from person to person and from accent to accent. The intonation with which a word is said can also affect the length of the glide. One person might pronounce the word 'shower' with just a long /ɑ:/ and another launch into the triphthong /aʊə/. The word 'player' might be pronounced /eɪə/.

SEMI-VOWELS /j/ and /w/

These two are difficult. Although they are used as consonants, they are made in the same way as vowels, with the air passing freely over the tongue.

Unrounded palatal semi-vowel /j/

The onset of this phoneme is in the half close and close areas of the vowel chart and the actual place of onset varies according to the following vowel. /ji:/ for example starts in a much closer position than /jɔ:/.

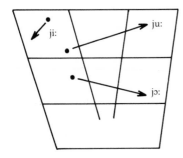

Labio-velar semi-vowel /w/

Here the vocalic glide starts in a velar, or back vowel, position and glides to the following vowel. Again the exact position of the glide varies. The /w/ may be devoiced by a preceding voiceless consonant, i.e. 'twin' and 'quick' [tw̥ɪn] and [kw̥ɪk]. The lips are more rounded when /w/ is followed by a back vowel than they are when it is followed by a front vowel. Compare 'wood' and 'week'.

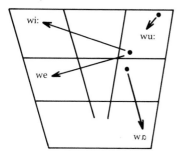

Fortis voiceless labio-velar fricative

Some English speakers use this fricative version of a 'w'. We often write these words with the letters 'wh', i.e. 'where', 'when', etc., but the sound is 'hwen', 'hwere', because of the extra friction in this realization of the phoneme.

Suggestions for further reading

Cotterell, G. (1977) *Diagnosis in the Classroom*, Reading, Centre for the Teaching of Reading.

Franklin, A. W. and Naidoo, S. (Eds) (1970) *Assessment and Teaching of Dyslexic Children*, London, The Invalid Children's Aid Association.*

Gimson, A. C. (1980) *An Introduction to the Pronunciation of English*, London, Edward Arnold.

Hornsby, B. and Shear, F. (1975) *Alpha to Omega*, London, Heinemann Educational.

Jesperson, O. (1948) *Growth and Structure of the English Language*, London, Basil Blackwell.

Miles, T. R. and Miles, E. (1983) *Help for Dyslexic Children*, London, Methuen.

O'Connor, J. D. (1973) *Phonetics*, Harmondsworth, Penguin.

Pollock, J. (1980) *Signposts to Spelling*, London, Heinemann Educational.†

Rak, E. T. (1972) *Spellbound*, Cambridge, Mass., Educators Publishing Service, Inc.‡

Rak, E. T. (1970) *Spell of Words*, Cambridge, Mass., Educators Publishing Service, Inc.‡

Steer, A., Peck, C. Z., and Kahn, L. (1971) *Solving Language Difficulties*, Cambridge, Mass., Educators Publishing Service, Inc.‡

*Available from The Invalid Children's Aid Association, 126 Buckingham Palace Road, London SW1.
†Also available from the Helen Arkell Dyslexia Centre, 15 Crondace Road, London SW6 4BB.
‡Available from Better Books, 15a Chelsea Road, Lower Weston, Bath BA1 3DU. (Although the spelling and pronunciation described in these books is American, they do contain much useful and adaptable material.)

Index